Nightmare on Grey Street
Newcastle's Darker Side

Vanessa Histon

Tyne Bridge Publishing

Acknowledgments:

This book was inspired by *A Walk on the Dark Side*, one of the excellent tours of Newcastle conducted by Newcastle's City Guides. Thanks are due to City Guides for allowing me to use their research as a starting point for my work. For further information about the City Guides contact Newcastle's Tourist Information Centre on 0191 2778000.

I should also like to thank the following people for information and advice: Jo Potts, Education Officer, Theatre Royal; Don Irving, Stage Doorman, Tyne Theatre; Brian Tempest, Tyneside Cinema; Michael Gibson, Manager, Old George Inn; Jessica Lee, Casa; Liz Peascod, Librarian, Literary and Philosophical Society; Bill Lowry; Anna Flowers, Tyne Bridge Publishing; Professor Norman McCord; Chris Mabbot; Frank Manders; Jimmy Donald; David Randall; Christopher Goulding; Julian Peck; Agnes & Dennis Chilton.

ISBN: 1857951905

Published by
City of Newcastle upon Tyne
Education & Libraries Directorate
Newcastle Libraries & Information Service
Tyne Bridge Publishing
2000

www.newcastle.gov.uk/tynebridgepublishing

Printed by Statex Colourprint, Newcastle upon Tyne

Front cover: Grey Street c.1890. The glass plate from which this photograph is reproduced is cracked.

INTRODUCTION

When people think about the past it tends to be with nostalgia. They fondly imagine a golden, happier, simpler age, bearing a striking resemblance to the merrier parts of the works of Charles Dickens. But for many people this simply was not the case. Life was often short, harsh and downright uncomfortable.

In the bright bustling commercial centre that is twenty-first century Newcastle, it is difficult to imagine that it was ever any different, but records and folklore preserve memories which show a darker side of the city. Whether the evidence is an official document recording the burial of a supposed witch, or the simple story of the ghost of a girl whose life was cut tragically short by illness, we are reminded that living in the past was sometimes a very dangerous thing to do.

CONTENTS

St Andrew's Church, Newgate Street, 1890. The oldest parts date back to the eleventh century. During the Civil War a gun was placed on the tower and there were no sermons or baptisms for a year.

GHOULS AND GHOSTS

Every collection of ghost stories should start with tales of haunted churchyards and spectral monks and nuns. Newcastle is rich in all of these.

ECCLESIASTICAL GHOSTS

The Sexton of St Andrew's

St Andrew's on Newgate Street is one of the four original parish churches of Newcastle (the others are St Nicholas's, All Saints', and St John's) and, as it is thought to date from the twelfth century, it could be the oldest. It has a leper's squint where people afflicted with this dreadful disease could watch mass without passing on their infection to the rest of the congregation. Leprosy is thought to have been brought to Britain by Crusaders returning from the Holy Land. The disease was greatly feared and sufferers, even people with unrelated but disfiguring skin diseases, were cut off from society. In Newcastle, the Hospital of St Mary Magdalene was founded at the beginning of the twelfth century at Barras Bridge on the site of the present St Thomas's Church. Here, outside the city walls, the lepers lived in the care of monks and nuns, and made their living by begging from pilgrims on their way to Jesmond. By the beginning of the sixteenth century, probably because of better standards of hygiene and diet, leprosy had disappeared from Britain.

St Andrew's has been altered and extended many times over the centuries. During the Civil War the Scots breached the town wall just beside the church and many townsfolk were killed. St Andrew's was so badly damaged that according to the parish register of 1645, there was neither baptism or sermon in the church for a year after the Scots took the town. The witch-hunting of those violent days is well recorded as fifteen people executed for witchcraft were buried at St Andrew's in 1650 (see page 21).

According to an old story, at the end of the eighteenth century a sexton of St Andrew's mysteriously disappeared in the middle of his day's work. Although they searched high and low for him, he wasn't found until the next day, lying at the bottom of a freshly dug grave, stone dead. People said at the time that he died of fright, but no one ever found out what had scared him so much. Perhaps he had seen some spectre from the church's chequered past.

There is a little truth at the root of this tale, although it does lack drama. According to *Sykes' Local Records*, on June 21 1765, the sexton of St Andrew's was found dead in a grave which he had been digging. Put in these terms, it seems much more likely that the cause of death was a heart attack rather than any supernatural manifestation.

Poor Charlotte

Nearly two hundred years ago, a young curate at St Andrew's church fell in love with Charlotte, the daughter of a wealthy landowner. They were happy for a while, but like so many lovers, they quarrelled and parted on bad terms. The curate couldn't stop thinking about his lost love, and one day decided to go and see her to try to win her back. As he was about to leave the church yard that evening, he caught sight of a girl in a blue muslin dress, just like Charlotte's favourite gown, moving among the gravestones. The girl turned and the

Thomas Oliver's map of Newcastle in the 1830s shows 'The Nuns', once belonging to St Bartholomew's Nunnery, and Anderson Place, which occupied the site of the old Grey Friars.

curate saw her face, and it was indeed his own sweet Charlotte. Overjoyed, he rushed towards her to beg her forgiveness, but she vanished among the tombs. Sadly, the curate went home, wondering why his sweetheart had apparently changed her mind after coming to seek him out.

The next day, the curate made another attempt to visit Charlotte at home. As he rode up to the house, he was startled to see that all the blinds were down. He was shown into a room where Charlotte's family were gathered, all in deepest mourning. Tearfully they told him that their precious Charlotte had died suddenly the previous evening, while wearing her favourite blue muslin gown.

If you pass St Andrew's, after dusk, and glimpse a flash of blue among the tombs, it could be the spirit of poor Charlotte, in her best muslin dress, trying to see her lost love for one last time.

The Nun of St Bartholomew's

The Benedictine nunnery of St Bartholomew was the oldest religious house in Newcastle, founded by 1135. It stood on the place now occupied by the Grainger Market, and, although it is difficult to imagine, this bustling area of the city once had vegetable and herb gardens and sheep and cows grazing on a green meadow – 'The Nuns', remembered in the name Nun Street. The daughters of royal and noble families received their education here. After the death of King Malcolm of Scotland, his queen's mother and sister, both English, fled from Scotland to the safety St Bartholomew's and took the veil there.

Eventually, St Bartholomew's was joined in Newcastle by other religious houses, Grey Friars

Black Friars on 12th August, 1883. In 1250 the Prior was accused of building extravagantly by his order of Dominican monks. After the Dissolution of the Monasteries the buildings were leased to Newcastle's craft companies and later became very run down. Perhaps the Prior haunts these now restored remains in protest at their disrespectful treatment by history.

(Franciscans) to the east and Black Friars (Dominicans) to the west. There were also Austin Friars and the White Friars (Carmelites) in medieval Newcastle. According to tradition, the Black Friars, Grey Friars and the nunnery were linked by secret underground passageways.

As in all the best stories, a monk from Black Friars fell in love with a nun from St Bartholomew's, during medieval times. Their clandestine affair was discovered when the nun became pregnant. As punishment for breaking her vows, she was walled up alive in the convent, a horrible death. Her spirit still walks the alley known as Nuns Lane.

We do not know how, or even if, the friar was punished, but a ghost has been seen in the cloisters of Black Friars (the remains of the monastery), disappearing through a wall.

Anderson Place was built in 1580 by Robert Anderson on the site of the old monastery of the Grey Friars. Sir William Blackett added to the building after 1675 and in 1782 Sir Thomas Blackett sold it to a builder, George Anderson, whose son named it Anderson Place. The house stood just off Pilgrim Street, approximately on the site of Lloyds bank, and the rear gardens adjoined 'The Nuns'.

The Phantom Film Fan

The Tyneside Cinema, on Pilgrim Street, stands on land which was once owned by the Grey Friars. For some years cleaners had been reluctant to work alone in the building early in the morning or late at night. They complained that cinema seats which had been left upright mysteriously folded themselves down again, they reported seeing a shadowy figure in dark robes and said they often felt inexplicably uneasy.

One member of staff at the cinema was particularly sceptical about these stories. He refused to believe that there was any kind of supernatural presence in the cinema until one Sunday evening in the early 1990s. He opened the door to the top floor cinema to prepare the auditorium for the evening screening. The room should have been empty, but he noticed a shadowy figure passing in front of the screen. Thinking it was a real person, he called to it and it vanished. He decided he had simply seen a shadow, but as he examined the room he found nothing that could cast a shadow in that shape.

Feeling cold and uncomfortable he went into the office and told his colleagues about his experience. Quite a few of them had similar stories to tell. Someone had seen a figure in flowing robes going into the finance office. Another member of staff reported standing in the upstairs cinema one evening when she felt the presence of *something* beside her. She could see no one, but clearly heard the sound of a man clearing his throat. Most of the staff agree that there is a very eerie feeling in the building.

STAGESTRUCK SPIRITS

Theatrical ghosts are almost as common as ecclesiastical hauntings. Newcastle's two oldest theatres boast a phantom each.

The Grey Lady of the Gallery

During the 1880s, a stagestruck lady used to visit the Theatre Royal on Grey Street to watch the performances from the gallery. At the end of each show she would go down to the stage door to collect autographs from the stars.

In this way she caught the eye of a leading actor of the day. She was overwhelmed by his attentions and fell madly in love with him. During the run of the show they were inseparable, and the actor promised the lady that they would elope together on the last night of the play.

The excited lady packed her bags and went to the stage door to wish her lover luck before his last performance. He asked her why she had brought her luggage. She replied that she was ready to start a new life with him whereupon the actor laughed in her face.

Sadly, not quite believing what had happened, the lady climbed the long staircase to the theatre gallery to watch her lover for one last time. When he came on to the stage, the lady stood up and held out her hand to him. Further and further she stretched out towards him until she overbalanced and toppled from the high gallery to her death. Her ghost, known as the Grey Lady, haunts the theatre to this day.

The archives of the Theatre Royal show that during the 1880s, the theatre boxes were actually closed for a while because someone had fallen from one of them. It is possible

The Theatre Royal, Grey Street, around 1890. The theatre was opened in 1836 replacing the old Theatre Royal which stood on Mosley Street.

Grey Street, 1890. This elegant street was constructed in the 1830s, and the Theatre Royal was built 1836-7. A fire in 1901 meant that the interior of the theatre had to be remodelled.

that the sad tale of lost love grew up around this fact, and that the story of the accident was transplanted from the boxes to the much higher gallery to increase the dramatic effect.

However the story of the Grey Lady arose, there are regular reports of mysterious happenings in the theatre. A stage electrician, opening the door of the gents, was embarrassed to see a lady standing in front of him. Thinking he'd gone to the wrong lavatory he quickly closed the door. No, he was in the right place after all. He opened the door again and the lady had vanished.

Another member of the theatre staff was working in one of the boxes when he heard a noise coming from the box above him. He went upstairs to investigate, but there was nothing there. Returning to his work, he was again disturbed by noise, and on his second visit upstairs found all the chairs in the box overturned. After that, he decided to lock himself into the lower box where he was working, just to be on the safe side, and to play his radio to block out any mysterious sounds.

The Tyne Theatre and Opera House, Westgate Road, c.1900.

The Cannonball and the Carpenter

Victorian stage managers knew that the best way to make a realistic thunder sound effect was to roll a cannonball down a length of battered tin guttering. Care had to be taken to angle the guttering correctly, as heavy cannonballs moving at speed could have a devastating effect in the confined area backstage. Robert Crowther, a stage carpenter at the Tyne Theatre on Westgate Road, was killed in 1887 when a 36lb cannonball fell

---

MONDAY, JUNE 30th, 1884,

AND DURING THE WEEK,

Will be Presented the Successful Three-Act Musical Comedy,

MY SWEETHEART.

The moral being pure and wholesome, the performance is worthy the patronage and consideration of every Parent. The story illustrating the difference between the love of a good girl and the fascination of a woman of the world.—*Standard.*

Adapted for the English Stage by FRED G. MAEDER.

Tina (with Songs, Dances, &c.) .... Miss MINNIE PALMER
Tony (with Songs, &c.) .... Mr. CHARLES ARNOLD
Joe Shotwell (a broken-down Sport)...........Mr. T. J. HAWKINS
Dr. Oliver (a true Friend) .... Mr. JOHN S. WOOD
Harold Bartlett (a Gambler) ...... Mr. GRAHAM WENTWORTH
Dudley Harcourt ("Dash it all") ... Mr. LAWRANCE D'ORSAY
Farmer Hatzell (a wealthy Farmer) .... Mr. GEORGE WRAY
Mrs. Fleeter (an Adventuress) .... Miss ELSIE CAREW
Mrs. Hatzell (the Farmer's Loving Wife).........Miss JANE GREY

From a Theatre Royal programme.

on him, fracturing his skull. Since then, his ghost has haunted the theatre.

Theatre staff call the ghost Bob. Bob seemed to have a liking for strangers, and it was usually members of visiting stage companies who would report seeing him. Regular members of the Tyne Theatre staff would just sense his presence. Staff would know when Bob was around because they could smell his pipe tobacco. Cleaners frequently reported that lights were switched on when there was no one in the vicinity. One lady who was selling merchandise in the foyer noticed a man in Victorian costume. There is a strict rule at the Tyne Theatre that actors must not appear in costume at the front of house, so the lady called to the man to reprimand him. To her surprise, the man disappeared.

In 1985 the stage at the Tyne Theatre was gutted by fire, and since that time Bob has not made his presence felt.

TWO SILKIES

A Silky is a female ghost, so called because she announces her presence with the rustle of her silk dress. The word may also have a connection with the northern (originally from Shetland) word 'Sealchie' meaning a supernatural spirit, usually in the form of a seal.

The Denton Hall Silky

East Denton Hall on the West Road out of Newcastle is an ancient place, a house on the site first appearing in the records during the sixteenth century, and some people say that parts of the existing hall were built with stone taken from the Roman Wall. As early as 1758 Elizabeth Montagu ('the queen of literary London' and friend of Samuel Johnson), a frequent visitor to the house which was owned at that time by Edward Montagu, claimed that rats and ghosts were in full possession of the house. She was probably describing the Silky, sometimes called the white lady, and known to the residents of the house as Old Barberry.

DENTON HALL.

East Denton Hall, built in 1622 for Dorothy and Anthony Errington. The house was occupied by various owners and in 1943 became the home of the Roman Catholic Bishop of Newcastle.

No one knows who the Silky was in life, but there is an ancient tradition of a girl being strangled by a jealous sister. Residents at the Hall became used to seeing her glide round in her white silk dress. She was usually described as gentle and caring, particularly when illness was in the house, when she would watch constantly until the invalid recovered. Some stories about the Silky are more alarming: on more than one occasion she frightened visitors so much that they left the house the next day, never to return. Another tale describes how the silky grasped the hand of a sleeping occupant of the Hall. The victim suffered pain in the hand for some time afterwards.

The Silky's influence was not confined to the Hall. Villagers around Denton claimed to hear her voice warning them of sickness and death, and pitmen in the area during the eighteenth century believed that she alerted them to impending danger in the mine.

At East Denton Hall the Silky rarely spoke, but she did make unearthly noises. One day in 1884 she was heard dragging something through two unoccupied rooms and down a flight of stairs to a window which she flung open.

The longest account of a visit from the Silky was written by a young lady who was a guest in the house at some time during the nineteenth century. The girl had spent the evening at a ball in the Old Assembly Rooms, in Newcastle. There she met a man whom she liked so much that 'our destinies were doomed to be connected'. Returning to the hall, she had gone to her room, locked the door and sat in front of the dressing table mirror preparing for bed.

Suddenly she felt another presence in the room, and looking round saw an elderly woman sitting on a nearby chair. The intruder was wearing a flowered satin gown and had large rings on her fingers. Her head was covered by a satin hood and she had deep, keen, penetrating eyes.

The old lady uttered her warning: 'So you have been to

An advertisement for the Old Assembly Rooms, c.1800. The Old Assembly Rooms were established on Westgate Road in 1776.

the ball tonight. I can see how happy you are, but if you knew what is known to me you would not pursue the romance.' Unhelpfully, she offered no explanation for this pronouncement. Then, as old ladies sometimes do, she took the opportunity to give a lengthy discourse on the follies and vanities of the age.

At the mention of vanity, the girl instinctively looked towards the mirror and was astonished to see that her visitor was not reflected in the glass. When she looked back at the chair there was no one there. She heard the rustle of silk and footsteps heading towards the door, but when she checked the

The doorway to East Denton Hall, dated 1622.

door it was locked, just as she had left it when she came home from the ball.

Very sensibly, the girl had her things removed from the room and spent the rest of her stay sleeping with her host's daughter. It would appear from the way she described the young man she had met at the ball that she ignored the old lady's warning and married him after all. History doesn't record whether or not they were happy.

In 1943 East Denton Hall became home to the Bishop of Hexham and Newcastle. Since his arrival the Silky has not appeared.

The Weary Widow

Martha Wilson, a seaman's widow lived in a room in the almshouses in the courtyard of Trinity House on Broad Chare, one of the widest of the narrow lanes leading off the Quayside. She was subject to fits of melancholy, and is reported to have threatened suicide on several occasions. On Sunday 13 April, 1817, she went out to buy a little tobacco. That was the last time she was seen alive. On the following Tuesday, she was found hanging from a beam in her room. The chair on which she had stood was overturned, her door key was lying on the floor and her prayer book lay open on her bed.

Suicides were denied burial in consecrated ground, and instead were laid to rest at a crossroads. Martha was buried at nightfall, on the public road leading from the New Bridge to the Red Barns near the buildings which were later called Ridley Villas. She was the last suicide in Newcastle to be buried at a crossroads. A large crowd of spectators watched the proceedings with morbid curiosity.

If reports from the 1860s are correct, an old custom made Martha's burial even more compellingly

The Quayside around 1900. The barrel-laden cart is just passing the entrance to Broad Chare.

gruesome. About fifty years after the suicide, the coroner, John Theodore Hoyle, was called to view the remains of a body which had been disinterred during excavations near Ridley Villas, in roughly the place where Martha had been laid to rest. He reported that the bones were found with a piece of wood in a position which indicated that a stake had been driven through the body.

If the stake had been intended to prevent Martha's spirit from walking among the living, it was unsuccessful. Not long after Martha's death, people walking near Broad Chare claimed to hear the rustling of a woman's dress and a soft chuckle. One night a Keelman was making his way home along the Quayside when he saw a woman on the other side of the road. She caught sight of him and, lifting her veil, beckoned him to approach. The Keelman wondered if he knew the woman. Her face was in shadow and he couldn't make out any features. As he drew nearer, he realised it wasn't quite so simple. He couldn't see any features, because the woman had no head.

Trinity House, c.1800, the home of the Guild of Masters and Mariners, one of the fifteen 'Bye-Trades' of the 'Free Incorporated Companies' of Newcastle. The site was purchased for the Guild in 1492 and it is still in use today. Broad Chare, to the right, in the early nineteenth century, was called 'broad' because it was wide enough for a cart to pass through.

CIVIL WAR GHOSTS: THE KING AND THE CAVALIER

Newcastle suffered greatly during the Civil War, so perhaps it is not surprising that two phantoms from those turbulent times have found a place in local folklore.

Charles I

After his defeat at Newark in 1646, King Charles I surrendered to the Scots and was brought to Newcastle. For ten months he was held in Anderson Place, a grand house with extensive gardens, which stood on the site now occupied by the Grey Street branch of Lloyds bank. The grounds of Anderson Place originally formed part of the Monastery of Grey Friars. On the dissolution of the monasteries the land passed into private hands and in 1580 Robert Anderson, a wealthy merchant built a noble mansion there.

For recreation King Charles was allowed to go to the Shieldfield to play goff (golf) and rested in a little house on Shieldfield Green which, unfortunately, was demolished as part of a redevelopment scheme in 1960.

Under the streets of modern Newcastle are many streams and burns which flow into the Tyne. In the seventeenth century, these streams flowed openly through the town. One is the Lort Burn, and it is claimed that boats were able to sail up it as far as Low Bridge. Legend has it that Charles I escaped by boat from Anderson Place, floating down the Lort towards the river. His freedom lasted only minutes and he was recaptured before reaching the river at Sandhill. Now his ghost is said to haunt the quayside, waiting for the rescue ship to return for him.

When Charles I made a state visit to Tynemouth in 1633, he was escorted by the Brethren of Trinity House. Perhaps it was this link which gave rise to the tale that, during the war, Charles hid for a time in a small cellar beneath the chapel at Trinity House. Financing the war was a constant source of worry for the King. Part of his income was a tax from coal

King Charles' House, Shieldfield Green, in 1960 before it was pulled down. No ghosts have been reported haunting the flats which occupy the site now.

shipped out of the Tyne and he is supposed to have spent much of his day looking through a squint in the wall of the buttress room, watching for ships and tallying his share.

The ghost of Charles I is said to walk Trinity House on certain nights. Perhaps he still frantically trying to balance his accounts. After a spate of robberies in the neighbourhood one of the Trinity House Brethren decided to keep watch all night. His vigil was disturbed, not by human intruders, but by the sound of doors constantly opening and shutting. Perhaps this was the spirit of the unhappy king.

The Spinning Cavalier of Sallyport Tower

This strangely named building was once part of Newcastle's fortifications. One story has it that it was called Sallyport because it was from there that troops would 'sally' forth on skirmishes during times of unrest, another claims that the name refers to a breach made in the wall during the time of the civil War siege.

The tower is said to be haunted by a Royalist who was killed during the siege of 1644. A number of people claim to have seen him. In one spectacular sighting, the cavalier rose to the ceiling, revolving as he went! It has been suggested that he was climbing a long demolished spiral staircase.

If you pass the tower as the sun is setting, look up at the window. Sometimes you can see the cavalier looking out over the town he fought and died for.

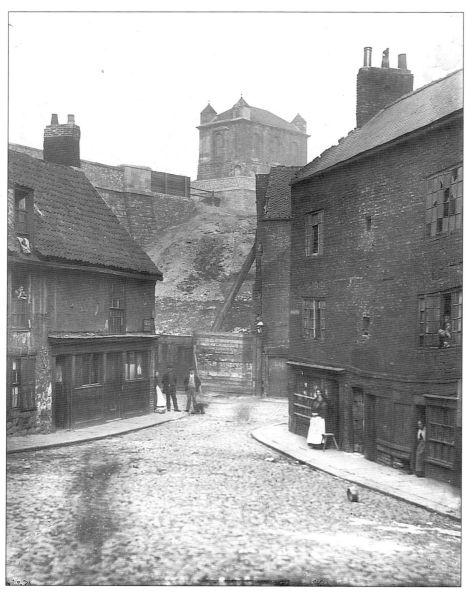

Sallyport Tower (also known as the Wall Knoll Tower) around 1880. The imposing building seen here was erected in 1716 by the Ships' Carpenters Company on the site of much Civil War fighting at the Town Wall. The old streets of Pandon have long been demolished.

INTOXICATING SPIRITS

It seems that there is more than one type of spirit to be found in some of Newcastle's pubs.

The Cooperage

The Cooperage public house and nightclub on the Close is a timber framed building dating from the sixteenth century and would originally have been home to a wealthy merchant. According to tradition, the timbers used to build it came from a ship which sank in the Tyne. Some of the bricks used in the construction are Dutch; perhaps they were brought over from the Netherlands as ships' ballast. Over the centuries the building was extended upwards because its proximity to the town wall meant that there was no room to build outwards. Every hundred years or so, a new storey was added.

Records show that in 1730 a cooper, or barrel maker, John Arthur, had premises in this area of the Quayside. In 1863 the business moved into the building now known as the Cooperage where it remained until 1973. After that the Cooperage was converted into a pub and restaurant. Perhaps because of its long history, it seems to be one of the most haunted buildings in Newcastle.

Disembodied chuckling, unexplained slamming doors and mysterious heavy footsteps from the upper rooms have all been reported at various times. There are frequent sightings of an elderly man who doffs his cap to ladies.

One night, during a quiet spell in the restaurant, a waiter sensed that someone had entered the room. He looked up to see a girl with long hair and odd looking clothes. She gazed wistfully at him for a few moments then vanished. No one knows who she

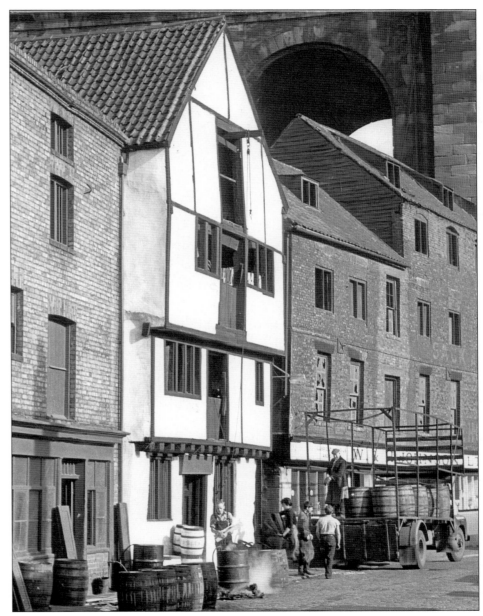

One of the oldest timber-framed buildings on the Close, the Cooperage, survives as a pub. This photograph dates from 1964.

was or why she was there, but since then she has often appeared in the restaurant. Some of the staff are so used to her that they ignore her and carry on with their work.

A more disturbing spirit haunts the building in the form of a smoke cloud. A member of staff working alone in the building late one night had a strange feeling of being watched. He turned around and saw a cloud of white smoke floating in the air. The room turned cold. Paralysed with fear, the man watched the cloud for a few helpless moments. As soon as he found the use of his legs he fled the building as fast as he could.

The cleaners were hard at work one day, when they heard a piercing, terrified scream coming from the function room. They rushed in and found one of their colleagues, who had been working alone there, shocked and sobbing with fear. She explained that she had caught a movement with the corner of her eye, and looking up, saw a luminous cloud forming at the end of the room. Like the man before her, she was too frightened to move and as she stared in horror she saw an arm and fist taking shape within the smoke. Slowly, the cloud began to move towards her. It was only when she has the presence of mind to scream for help that the apparition vanished.

Left: Broad Chare c.1890. The building on the right with the projecting beam is Arthur's Cooperage.

Watergate Building

Not far from the Cooperage is the Swing Bridge. The building on the east side of the bridge was designed by John Dobson and is known as Watergate Building. Formerly the Dagliesh shipping office, in recent years it has had various identities as a bar and restaurant.

In 1993, when it was known as Hanrahan's, strange things began to happen. Regulars reported seeing spectral figures in corridors. Glasses were rearranged and staff felt as though they were being watched. One customer met a formless shadowy apparition, which seemed to be watching him from a toilet cubicle.

At the time of writing the restaurant is called Casa. Staff are often uneasy about being in the building late at night or early in the morning. Stairs in the bar lead to a basement room known as the crypt and sometimes strange noises come from the crypt when no one is in that part of the building.

It is interesting that the basement is called the crypt, because Watergate buildings stands in the site of the ancient Bridge Chapel of St Thomas The Martyr. First mentioned in records in 1248, the chapel sat on the line of the medieval Tyne Bridge, remains of which can still be seen in the basement. The chapel was demolished in 1830 and St Thomas's church at Barras Bridge was built to replace it.

The Old George

The Old George Inn off the Cloth Market is haunted by a ghost known to the staff as 'Charlie' who had his own special chair in the bar. According to tradition, when Charles I was imprisoned in Newcastle he sometimes stopped off to drink at the Old George after playing golf. Presumably Charlie the ghost is yet another manifestation of the dead king. Charlie was usually quiet and friendly until the day in 1977 when his chair was taken away for repair. He became a very cross ghost indeed. Cleaners would hear a voice coming from an empty room, and footsteps furiously pacing the upper floor. Doors would lock mysteriously and cigarette packets would be scattered around the bar when there was no one there. In Charlie's most spectacular display of temper, a clock jumped off the wall and flew several feet across the room.

The old chapel of St Thomas the Martyr which was pulled down in 1830. The chapel, and its crypt, stood on the site of the Watergate Building.

Unsurprisingly, after that it never worked again.

Charlie hasn't been seen or heard from recently, but over the last few years there have been several sightings of a female ghost. She is a woman in a long black dress who appears at the top of the stairs. Sometimes, when she realises she has been seen, she runs back up the stairs towards the old attic bedrooms. On one occasion a customer had seen the ghost in the pub and came back the following afternoon to tell the manager about his experience. As they stood chatting at the bottom of the stairs, an almighty commotion came from the upper floor. It sounded exactly like ten or twelve women shouting. A search revealed that the upper floor was empty, and when the men went into the bar they discovered that there were no women at all in the building that afternoon.

The Old George in 1924, at a low point in its long career as a public house.

The most recent sighting of the woman in black was just before Christmas, 1999. A customer was in the ladies' room, chatting to a woman in a black dress. Abruptly the woman exclaimed 'I must go upstairs' whereupon she vanished.

SPIRITS OF INDUSTRY

Ancient buildings are the most romantic settings for hauntings, but ghost stories can arise even in a busy workplace.

The Spectre of Shop 17

In November 1975, a crane driver going on night shift at Vickers Elswick works met a man he assumed to be a gaffer, dressed in old fashioned clothes. He didn't recognise the man, but greeted him anyway, then started to climb up to the cab of the High Flyer crane. Minutes later, the terrified driver felt unseen hands trying to push him out of the cab.

As the story spread round the works, other tales of mysterious happenings in shop 17 began to emerge. Shop 17 had been closed for several years, and since its reopening in 1974, two other workers had seen a little man in a bowler hat. A patrolman going through the shop had felt hands trying to hold him back when there was no one there. Then people remembered that in the 1950s there had been a number of reports of a mysterious shadow on the wall of shop 17.

Eventually the phenomena were blamed on a Vickers foreman who had disappeared in the 1930s. His clothes were found on the river bank. It was presumed that he had been disappointed in love and had jumped into the river and drowned.

The main entrance to Vickers Elswick works on Scotswood Road in 1969. The Elswick Works was started in 1847 as W.G. Armstrong & Co. and was merged with Vickers in 1927-1928. By the 1950s there were seventy acres of engineering shops, machine shops and foundries.

The Immaterial Mason

Another working ghost astounded west end residents in the mid-nineteenth century. Richard Lowry, a man who lived in Newcastle and kept a detailed diary for many years, recorded on 20 December, 1841:

> *I forgot to mention that 2 or 3 days ago a Ghost has made its appearance in Newcastle. It is the spectre of a mason who recently died in Westgate Street. It seems that he had not quite finished with his work before he died but came back to complete it. A noise as of a man at work has been heard in his room for several nights after he was buried. Hundreds congregated on the spot each night.*

Lowry was sceptical about such superstitions, but was still curious enough to to try to see the ghost for himself. He added:

I went one night, anxious to have a sight of this immaterial mason but was not fortunate enough to do so.

The Phantom in the Library

The Literary and Philosophical Society on Westgate Road has the oldest surviving independent library in Newcastle. Readers enjoy the peaceful and relaxed atmosphere and the wonderful range of books. One member of staff loved it so much that it seems he was reluctant to leave, even after his death. He is thought to be T. H. Marr, who was sub-librarian from 1893 until his death in 1930. Since then, his genial spirit has haunted the library, obviously still passionate about reading. He has made his presence felt very recently.

The Literary and Philosophical Society Library c.1930, when the ghost of Librarian T.H. Marr possibly took up residence. The appearance of the building has changed very little since those days.

One day the caretaker was working in the reference room. He clearly heard the pages of a book being turned in the next cubicle. When he looked in to see who was reading, the caretaker found the cubicle empty.

On another dark evening, the librarian was preparing to lock up the building for the night when she met a very shaken and frightened assistant. She had felt a strange presence in the reference room. The librarian tried to calm her but as they passed the Reading Room, both of them felt that someone else was there, and both saw a shadowy figure. Perhaps it was just the spirit of Mr Marr eager to bid them goodnight and continue his reading in peace.

WITCHES AND WARLOCKS

THE GREAT WITCH TRIAL

By the middle of the seventeenth century, witch fever was raging through Europe. A verse from the biblical *Exodus*, 'Thou shalt not suffer a witch to live' sanctioned the denunciation and death of hundreds of women – and men – whose only crimes were eccentricity, unpopularity, or perhaps inconveniently owning a coveted piece of land.

On 26 March, 1649, a witchfinder named Kincaid was summoned by the magistrates and officials of Newcastle to seek out the servants of Beelzebub. His unprecedented success in identifying witches could perhaps be explained by the fact that he was paid twenty shillings for each one convicted, at a time when the average wage was around sixpence a day.

Newcastle's town bellman, Walter Dees, went round the streets calling on the citizens to denounce any witch. Opportunistic neighbours managed to produce thirty suspects who were rounded up and taken to the Guildhall for examination.

The accused often had their clothes pulled up and were examined for witch marks. Any tiny mole or blemish was enough to prove their guilt. Another way of proving a witch was to sink a pin into her flesh. If she did not bleed, she was guilty. Of course, as witchfinders used special pins with retractable points, guilt was usually certain.

Not everyone present at the trial believed wholeheartedly in Kincaid's skills. Lieutenant Colonel Hobson was deputy governor of Newcastle and an elder of the Baptist community. He also, apparently, had an eye for a pretty face. When a beautiful woman was brought before the court, Hobson exclaimed 'Surely! This woman is none and need not be tried.' Kincaid promised to prove she was a witch. In front of the crowd, he grabbed the woman's skirts and dragged them over her head, leaving her naked to the waist. She was so shocked, frightened and ashamed that she could not utter a word in her defence and failed to bleed

The old Guildhall occupied part of the fifteenth century hospital of the Maison Dieu (House of God) during the seventeenth century when witch trials were held here. The building was finally pulled down in 1823, when this drawing was made by the artist T.M. Richardson.

when Kincaid pushed his pin into her thigh. Hobson was sceptical and declaring that fear had prevented her bleeding, demanded that the woman be pricked again. This time the blood rushed forth and Kincaid forfeited his 20 shillings.

Other defendants were not lucky enough, or perhaps not pretty enough, to be saved by Hobson. One wizard and fourteen witches were hanged on the Town Moor in August, 1650. (Witches were burned in Scotland, but hanged in England). The parish register of St Andrew's church records

'these partes her undernamed were executed in the town mor for witches – Isabella Brown, for a wich; Margrit Maddeson, for a wich; Ann Watson, for a wich; Ellenor Henderson, for a wich; Ellenor Rogers, for a wich; Ellsabeth Dobson, for wich; Mathew Boumer, for a wich; Ellsabeth Anderson, for a wich; Jane Hunter, for a wich; Jane Koupling, for a wich; Margrit Brown, for a wich; Margrit Moffot, for a wich; Ellenor Robson, for stealing silver spounes; Kattren Welsh, for a wich; Ayles Hume, for wich; Mary Pootes, for a wich.'

They were buried in St Andrew's churchyard at a cost of sixpence a grave. This sum included the price of the iron rivets driven into the knees of the corpses to prevent them walking after death.

Kincaid the witchfinder moved north, tempted by promise of richer pickings of anything up to £3 per witch. In Scotland, by an ironic twist of fate, he fell foul of the law and was himself tried as a witch. After admitting that his fraudulent methods had caused the deaths of 220 innocent people (and earned him around £1,000 in fees), he was condemned to death.

Although Kincaid was discredited, witch trials continued in Newcastle. One of the more outrageous was that of Dorothy Stranger who, it was claimed, sometimes appeared in the form of a cat. In 1663 Jane Milburne snubbed Dorothy Stranger by failing to invite her to a wedding supper. Dorothy swore she would make Mistress Milburne regret the insult. After that

Jane was beset by cats at every turn. One appeared to her while she was alone in her chamber, another leapt at her throat while she was dressing for church. A third knocked her down on the stairs and kept her there for about quarter of an hour without power of her body or tongue. At the same time, Jane was also tormented by Dorothy in her human shape. She appeared mysteriously in a locked cellar, she nipped and bit Jane while she was in bed.

In 1664, claimed Mistress Milburne, she saw a grey cat transform before her very eyes into Dorothy Stranger. The witch flew at her, cutting and scratching her until she drew blood. Then she vanished.

It would seem that this evidence was simply too fanciful to convince the court. Cannon Raine, who researched witch trials for the Surtees Society, observed that he had in no instance discovered the record of the conviction of a reputed witch. Dorothy Stranger went free, along with Jane Simpson, a fruit seller, charged in 1644 of causing fits in a woman who had accused her of overcharging, and Mrs Pepper, a healer who, probably rashly, claimed that the breath of young children would draw the evil spirits out of people suffering from illness.

Black Jacky Johnson

Around 1820, if any of the good people of Newcastle had a problem and a few spare coins, they could consult Black Jacky Johnson, professor of the black arts, who lived on Dog Bank. Black Jacky could tell fortunes, charm warts and divine future husbands.

Dog Bank c.1880. Black Jacky lived in one of the forty-nine dwellings on this narrow lane.

A particular service he offered, and one much in demand, was to use his magic mirror to find stolen property. Such was his reputation for success that the mere threat of looking in Jacky's mirror was often enough to ensure that the stolen goods were mysteriously and secretly returned to their owner.

Black Jacky had a grisly spell for invisibility; those of a sensitive disposition are advised to skip the next paragraph.

First find a black cat without a single white hair on its body. On a Sunday, during the time of divine service, boil the cat for three hours. Take the cat's heart and dry it in an oven, never before used, until it is reduced to a fine powder. Conceal the powder in a churchyard, and visit it each night at precisely midnight, for seven consecutive nights. On the seventh night you will meet another who will walk with you to the churchyard gate. You must give him half the powder, as soon as you arrive, to protect yourself from certain destruction. The rest of the powder is yours, and forever after, whenever you carry it you will remain invisible.

A less elaborate spell, probably more popular with Black Jacky's regular customers, was for the curing acne:

Go to the sea, and collect as many pebbles as you have spots. Put the spots in a cloth bag and leave it at a crossroads. If a passer by picks up the bag, he will inherit your spots and you will be cured.

It wasn't long before Black Jacky's reputation as a sorcerer came to the attention of the authorities. He was hounded out of town and went to live in Byker. Presumably the people there were more tolerant – or more afraid of his powers – because he continued to practise the black arts. In fact, when he died in 1837, he was in the middle of reading the tarot cards. The story has it that he remained motionless in his chair for several days before finally toppling over.

Black Jacky left his books to the people of Newcastle – but where they are now is not known.

THE BODYSNATCHERS

From the mid-eighteenth century the study of medicine began to be more scientific, and a knowledge of anatomy was essential for any practitioner wishing to learn the new advances in surgery. Unfortunately at this time there were strong religious and moral objections to the dissection of the human cadaver, and only the bodies of criminals were allowed to be used in this manner. This meant that demand for corpses by the medical schools far outstripped the supply. In fact the famous Scottish surgeon, John Hunter, claimed he had to gain his understanding of the human nervous system from the body of a dog.

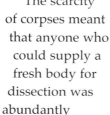

The scarcity of corpses meant that anyone who could supply a fresh body for dissection was abundantly rewarded and not too closely questioned about the source. Over the next few decades a new and grisly trade sprang up – digging up fresh corpses, only hours after burial, and selling them on to the anatomists. In Edinburgh (a great centre for medical education, where demand was particularly high) Burke and Hare ensured a steady income for themselves by actually murdering victims, rather than simply reclaiming the newly dead.

In 1832 the Anatomy Act allowed medical schools to use any unclaimed corpses, not just criminals, once 48 hours had elapsed. This law put the bodysnatchers out of business, but not before their gruesome trade had reached Newcastle.

Strange Deliveries at the Turf Hotel

The Turf Hotel, which stood on the site of the Allied Irish bank on Collingwood Street, was the most important coaching inn in the North of England. Packages arrived there to be forwarded to all corners of the country. Sometimes packages missed the last coach on Saturday and were stored in the booking office over the weekend until they could be dispatched on Monday.

One Monday in September 1825, staff opened up the booking office to discover a foul stench coming from one of the boxes which had been stored there since Saturday evening. Alarmed, they called the police and a magistrate who opened the box to discover the decomposing body of a young woman.

The girl appeared to have died from natural causes and, because there was no identification on her body, she was buried in a pauper's grave. The box, which would never have been discovered had it caught the last coach on Saturday, had been addressed to a James Syme, 6 Forth Street, Edinburgh. Edinburgh was, of course, home of the great medical schools.

After that, staff at the Turf Hotel were very suspicious of any package more than four feet long. On the night of January 26, 1826, a large box arrived in Newcastle by the Telegraph coach from Leeds. The box weighed more than 16 stones. The police were sent for immediately. The box was addressed to Mr Simpson at 61 Princes Street, Edinburgh. Inside was the body of a man, over 6 feet tall, between 40 and 50 years old,

Collingwood Street, 1848, a very early photograph showing the scene of the bodysnatching scandal at the Turf Hotel. None of the original three-storey buildings are left today, including the infamous hotel.

The Turf Hotel on Collingwood Street seems to have been involved in a bodysnatching enterprise.

large boned, with dark hair and an aquiline nose. The corpse was not yet putrid. An inquest was not able to determine the cause of death and found no traces of violence on the body.

A further body arrived on the coach from York in 1828. In the same year, another suspicious box was brought to the hotel by an Edinburgh man named James Aitcheson. Wary staff opened the box, a corpse was discovered, and Aitcheson was immediately arrested. Somehow, he managed to convince the police that he was ignorant of the contents of the box, and he was released.

The next day, a shopkeeper told police that he had sold Aitcheson the materials needed to make the box. It was obvious that Aitcheson was not as innocent as he claimed. The police and magistrates, hugely embarrassed, hastily issued a

warrant for Aitcheson's arrest, but of course he had vanished from the town.

The Turf Hotel was certainly a staging point in a grisly supply chain. The sensational trial of Burke and Hare revealed that Hare had been in Newcastle in 1828. It is interesting to speculate that he was in some way involved in the transportation of corpses via the Turf hotel.

The Body from Byker

The Queen's Head was another coaching inn, standing on the site of St Cuthbert's Inn, a hostelry for medieval pilgrims. The building stands on the west side of Pilgrim Street, and is now known as Alderman Fenwick's house.

After the dreadful happenings at the Turf Hotel, staff at the Queen's Head treated all long packages with suspicion. On Thursday January 8, 1829, a man with a soft Scottish accent deposited a box in the booking office. When it was opened, the staff were horrified to find the body of a child, Lizzie Mills, a shoemaker's daughter, who had been buried in Byker just that week.

Police rushed to the graveyard and were astonished to find that there were very few signs of disturbance at the grave. The bodysnatchers were so skillful that they could disinter a body without detection.

The Tale of the Bad Beadle

Although the Anatomy Act put the bodysnatchers out of business, grave robbing re-emerged in Newcastle almost a quarter of a century later.

After the cholera epidemic of 1853, sanitary regulations forbade burials in the churchyards of Newcastle's four parish churches. This had a devastating effect on the beadle of All Saints. One of his duties was digging graves and if there were no graves to dig, there was no money to be made.

In 1858, he hit upon a cunning plan to supplement his dwindling fortunes. Late at night he would steal into the churchyard, and by the light of a lantern, he would open a grave and steal the lead lining from the coffin. He didn't realise that his flickering lantern could be seen by people living in the houses in Silver Street.

At first this worked in his favour. People assumed that the mysterious light was a supernatural manifestation and kept well clear of the churchyard at night. Then, for some reason, perhaps because the beadle was selling suspicious amounts of lead, an investigation was mounted. When it was discovered that some graves in the churchyard had been violated a watch was set and the beadle was caught red handed.

The beadle was tried at the Guildhall in front of Mr Justice Keating, and was sentenced to eighteen months hard labour. The people were incensed at his crime and at what they considered the lenience of his sentence (actually, the maximum the law allowed) and he had to be very carefully guarded as he was removed from court, or the mob would have torn him to pieces. For many years afterwards the street lads used to sing:

All Saints Church around 1890. Silver Street is to the rear.

31

Silver Street, overlooking All Saints graveyard c.1890.

If you want to rob the dead
Gan tae Jack the beadle
He's the one who stole the lead
Pop goes the weasel

This wasn't the first time that those sleeping in All Saints churchyard had been disturbed. On the night of 7 January, 1802, 60-70 feet of the church yard wall collapsed, falling into Silver Street and knocking in the doors and windows of the houses. When the terrified householders emerged to find out the cause of the damage, they were greeted by the grisly sight of coffins and bones which had been exposed by the cave-in.

The Bigg Market and a few of its many pubs in 1880.

Death of a Miser

One rather dubious story connected with robbing the dead goes that an old man died without making provision in his will for all the trappings considered proper at a funeral. As the funeral procession trailed up the Bigg Market to the graveyard at St John's, his unwilling friends and relatives baulked at the thought of sitting through a long funeral service for such a miserable man. One by one, they slipped away from the procession and into one of the Bigg Market's many pubs.

Eventually only the vicar and the coffin bearers were left. Realising that none of the relatives cared a jot what happened to the old man, the bearers turned smartly about and headed for the Barber Surgeons' Hall, where they sold both coffin and corpse for beer money. Only the vicar walked on towards the church, his mind on higher things.

The Barber Surgeons' Hall where bodies were much in demand for anatomy instruction.

MURDER AND MAYHEM

THE DUEL AT THE WHITE CROSS

The White Cross used to stand on Newgate Street near the entrance to Low Friar Street. It first appears in the records in 1410. Several markets were held between the Newgate and the White Cross. It was also the scene of an infamous duel.

In 1701 Ferdinando Forster, MP and John Fenwick of Rock, coal owner, were attending a Grand Jury dinner at the Black Horse Inn, near the crossroads of Clayton Street and Newgate Street. There was great rivalry between the two men who started to argue. Friends intervened and calm was restored … until the next morning when Forster and Fenwick met accidentally at the White Cross.

They resumed their argument, hurling verbal abuse at each other until a crowd gathered. The mob, anxious to see a fight, urged the contenders ever more towards violence until eventually swords were drawn. The two men were well matched, but Forster slipped and fell. Fenwick seized his opportunity, ran his opponent through and fled towards Gallowgate.

Within a week Fenwick was arrested, tried and executed. Usually hangings took outside the city walls, but the authorities were afraid that the pitmen employed by Fenwick at Kenton would try to rescue him. Instead the town gates were closed and Fenwick was hanged from a white thorn tree growing near the scene of his crime.

Also at the White Cross stood the pillory where people convicted of trivial offences were confined in great discomfort, the target for rotten vegetables and the ridicule of their neighbours.

One woman, Susanah Fleming, nearly suffered a much worse fate. Convicted of fortune telling in April 1758, she was sentenced to be pilloried for just one hour every quarter for a year. Perhaps she fainted on one occasion, but somehow she was slowly being strangled. Eventually a sailor in the crowd noticed her plight and climbed up to rescue her. He brought her down the ladder on his back, more dead than alive.

The Secret Life of Archie Bolam

In the early hours of 7 December 1838, the fire brigade were called to the savings bank in the Royal Arcade. Smoke was pouring from an inner room. Firemen broke into the room and were confronted by a sickening scene. Blood, brains and hair spattered the carpet and furniture. In the midst of the gore, one man lay dead, another, seemingly, half dead.

The dead man was Joseph Millie, clerk of the bank and a man of impeccable character. His skull had been smashed with a poker, then his pockets were filled with coals and paper and set alight. Presumably, the murderer hoped that the blaze would hide evidence of the crime.

The other man was Archie Bolam, an actuary and highly respected bank official. He said that while working at the bank the previous evening he had received the latest in a series of threatening letters which had been sent to him over the preceding weeks. He decided to go home to Gateshead and warn his housekeeper, Mary Walker, to be on her guard against intruders.

When he returned to the bank he saw Millie lying on the hearthrug. Believing Millie to be asleep (despite the scene of carnage surrounding him) he went to his desk and opened the lid. Suddenly a man with a blackened face struck him on the right temple. Bolam ran shouting to the windows, but the intruder threatened to kill him as he had done Millie. He knocked Bolam to the ground and tried to cut his throat. Bolam passed out, only regaining consciousness when the firemen arrived.

Perhaps Bolam's story was just a little too elaborate. It certainly was not true. The firemen suspected him immediately. Bolam had opened his eyes as soon as they entered the room, but shut them again quickly to give the impression of unconsciousness. There was no sign of an intruder at the bank, nor any way he could have gained access to the building. Despite the appalling amount of blood in the room, there was none on the floor where Bolam lay. Bolam's wounds did not correspond to the damage to his clothes, and the cut on his throat was not deep enough to point to a serious attempt at murder. A bloodied paper knife on a nearby desk seemed likely to be the weapon which had inflicted the wound.

Left, Archie Bolam, murderer; right, Joseph Millie, victim.

Bolam was tried for the murder of Joseph Millie. Although the prosecution did not offer a motive for the murder, speculation outside the courtroom was rife. It was rumoured that that the respectable Bolam regularly frequented vice dens and gaming houses. His housekeeper was, in fact, his mistress. He had been embezzling funds from the bank to finance his decadent lifestyle. A newspaper article written decades after the murder described him as:

A morbid and self-tormenting sensualist, a hypocrite of a particularly vile kind, and one who … held communion with filthy and depraved characters.

The turning point of the trial came when Walker, the housekeeper, admitted that when Bolam had returned home, ostensibly to warn her of intruders, he had asked her to sponge his clothes. The clothes were then produced in court, and when examined disclosed blood stains and smears. The prosecution claimed that Bolam had murdered Millie, gone home to remove as much of the evidence as possible from his person, and returned to the bank to set the scene for his alibi. The evidence was suggestive, certainly, but not enough to hang a man. Judge Maule directed the jury to find Bolam

The sad remains of the once sumptuous Royal Arcade on Pilgrim Street in the 1950s. The ghost of Joseph Millie might well have been seen here at the scene of his murder.

The Royal Arcade pictured in 1888.

The scene at the Savings Bank on the night of the murder.

at his office at 2 Blackett Street and stopped to talk to a friend. It was to be Frater's last conversation.

As they chatted a man approached, who, without warning, grabbed Frater with one hand and stabbed him viciously in the neck with a table knife. According to a contemporary account:

The savage determination of the murderer may be judged from the circumstances that his weapon entered an inch or two from the right corner of the mouth, inflicting a savage gash on the cheek, glancing past the bone and severing all the main arteries in the neck.

The murderer wrenched the knife round in the wound, actually twisting the blade in the process, then withdrew it and stood in silence to watch the last agonies of his victim.

Frater somehow managed to get to his office. He collapsed into a chair, whispering 'I am done for' to his clerk. He was losing blood rapidly and quickly passed out. Within ten minutes he was dead.

The assailant was George Clark, an unmarried 45 year old chair maker who lived at St Nicholas Churchyard. He had previous convictions for assault. Clark was seized by two witnesses and taken to the police station. He showed no remorse:

'Decidedly so, I murdered him. He robbed me, now I've robbed him. This is a grand day for the penny papers, they'll have a grand sale today.'

At Clark's trial at the Guildhall it emerged that Clark had refused to pay his six shilling dog license fee. Frater had the power to confiscate property to the value of the debt, but Clark tried to avoid this by selling all his tools for cash and finding an employer who would provide tools for him. He constantly brooded over the dog license and is quoted as saying 'I will blow their brains out if they come again for the money.' As his debt increased, Clark risked losing his home and blamed Frater for his ruin. Over the months his hatred for

innocent of willful murder. Instead, he was convicted of manslaughter and sentenced to life transportation to Australia.

Bolam went to Australia and prospered. He worked as a schoolteacher, a commission agent and collector of debts. He also held a responsible position in the church, collecting pew rents and dealing with other matters. He apparently 'enjoyed great confidence from all classes as a good and honest man, notwithstanding a somewhat peculiar manner.' As a mark of his respectability regained he even presented a sundial to the Botanical gardens in Sydney.

Bolam died still protesting his innocence. On his tombstone in St Stephen's, Sydney, is the inscription 'Here lies an honest man'.

The Blackett Street Murder

Mark Frater was a tax collector who lived in Bulman's Village near Gosforth. On the morning of October 1, 1861, he arrived

Blackett Street at the turn of the century.

Frater grew and twisted inside him, until it exploded in a frenzied, murderous attack.

Clark was sentenced to death, but then doubts were cast on his sanity. He escaped the scaffold but was sent to Broadmoor where he was regarded as one of the most dangerous inmates. Mark Frater is buried in Jesmond Old Cemetery.

The Corpse in the Midden

Before Richard Grainger's development of the 1820s, the area where Blackett Street and Old Eldon Square now stand was unwholesome and dotted with pigsties, manure heaps and rubbish dumps. One day when some workmen were carrying away some of the manure, they discovered a child's body buried in the heap.

A coroner and jury were hastily assembled. One of the jurymen cautiously prodded the corpse and pronounced 'that the body was in a putrid state'. Of course it was, it had just been pulled out of a midden!

Next to examine the body was the Coroner who was a surgeon. His trained medical eye immediately honed in on the fact that the corpse was nothing more than a wooden doll. Then someone remembered that when Stephen Kemble retired as manager of the Theatre Royal in Mosley Street, he had cleared out lots of stage props from his house in Newgate Street. This doll, which had once appeared in a play, had just taken part in its final and most dramatic performance.

This view shows the area around Pilgrim Street, and the as yet unconstructed Blackett Street in 1702. At that time the Blackett family were living in the mansion which they had built on the site of the Grey Friars monastery. The Nuns' Field lies beyond, within the town walls. Over a century later this central part of the town was to be redeveloped by Richard Grainger, and the pigsties on the north side of the lane leading to Newgate became the elegant gardens of Eldon Square.

THE GALLOWS WALK

HALF-HANGED MCDONALD

Ewan McDonald was a recruit in the Regiment of Highlanders. One night in 1752, McDonald, then aged 19, was drinking in Pinkey's ale house in the Bigg Market. A fellow drinker, Robert Parker, a cooper, was making anti-Scottish jokes. McDonald took offence and a fight broke out. Parker was stabbed in the neck and died and McDonald was tried and sentenced to hang.

On the day of the execution, McDonald was in a fighting fury. When the executioner attempted to place the noose around his neck, McDonald lashed out with his feet, knocking the hangman from the scaffold. The hangman dusted himself down and climbed back up, and finally sent McDonald to meet his maker. Or so everyone thought …

McDonald's body hung on the scaffold for the prescribed amount of time, then was cut down and brought to the barber surgeons for dissection. The young medical student charged with looking after the room was busy with his duties when he heard a groan coming from the corner. He looked round and was horrified to see McDonald sitting up and begging for mercy. What should he do? As we have already seen, corpses for dissection were hard to come by. The student really did not want to allow one to climb off the slab and escape. Moreover, he reasoned, McDonald was already a dead man in the eyes of the law. So, seizing a heavy mallet, he swung it at Mcdonald's head and finished the executioner's job. That would be something to boast about to his friends – no one could charge him with killing a dead man!

Young students should not play God, and retribution was swift and sure. The student was going into the stables when a frisky horse kicked him on the head. The student died instantly. Some people claimed that the horse was possessed by the spirit of McDonald, taking revenge for that fatal blow.

In another version of the story, the student took pity on McDonald and let him go free. McDonald crept into the stables to find a horse to make his escape, the horse reared, kicked him on the head and killed *him*. MacDonald's body was found, taken back to the dissecting rooms and the surgeons got their corpse after all.

The Man They Couldn't Hang

Much luckier than McDonald was John Lee, a footman. He had been sentenced to death at Exeter for murdering his employer. On February 23, 1885 he mounted the scaffold, the

The Chancellor's Head, 1964, before demolition.

seventy-inch long noose which failed to hang Lee has recently gone up for auction.

Gin-soaked Jin

Jane Jamieson (sometimes spelled Jameson), known as Jin, was a fish hawker, renowned for drunkenness and rowdy behaviour. On New Year's day, 1829, Jin was drinking with her companion, William Ellison, known as Billy Elly, when they ran out of money. In a furious temper, Jin went to see her mother who lived at the Keelmen's Hospital. She demanded money, her mother refused, and a terrible fight broke out. When the mother accused Jin of murdering her father and two illegitimate children, Jin grabbed the red hot poker from the fire and ran it through her mother's body.

Jin was tried on March 5, 1829. The court was packed for this sensational case. At first she had tried to blame Billy Elly for the murder claiming that he had kicked her mother to death with his hob nailed boots. Presumably, a red hot poker leaves very different forensic evidence from hob nailed boots but Ellison could also prove that he had gone nowhere near the house but had stayed behind at the inn when the murder was being committed. Suspicion passed from him. At the trial Jin admitted 'I must

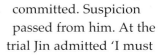

Jane Jamieson on March 5th 1829 on trial for her life at the Guildhall.

executioner put the noose round his neck, pulled the lever and the trapdoor failed to drop. Lee remained standing there for seven minutes, patiently waiting to be launched into eternity. Again the hangman tried, and again. When the trapdoor failed for the third time, Lee was thought to have suffered enough and his sentence was commuted to life imprisonment. After twenty-one years he came to Newcastle to start a new life.

Mr Wears, owner of the Chancellor's Head on Newgate Street gave Lee a job as barman. Mr Wears was an astute businessman. Lee was paid £8 a week, a considerable sum, but his value to the pub was enormous. Customers came from far and near, keen to see the man who had cheated the hangman three times. A privileged few were permitted to shake his hand.

Lee was very kind to the Wears' young son, but Mrs Wears was terrified of him. She met him only once and promptly fainted, unnerved by his hard piercing eyes. Lee emigrated to America in 1917 and died there in 1933. Coincidentally the have done it, I was too drunk to remember.' She was found guilty and sentenced to be hanged the following Saturday.

The execution attracted even more of a crowd than the trial. After all, Jin was the first woman to be publicly hanged in Newcastle for 71 years. The *Newcastle Courant* reported:

> *The crowd that attended the execution was immense. We have heard the number of persons estimated at 20,000, more than half of whom were women. The dreadful ceremony does not seem to have made on all who witnessed it the impression it should have made, for there were some pockets picked at the time.*

Jin's body was taken to the Barber Surgeons' where it was put on public display before being plunged in a vat of boiling water and flayed. John Fife delivered anatomical lectures on the corpse for several days before it was finally dissected.

A young surgeon's assistant, Thomas Giordani Wright, attended most of the lectures. He reported:

> *Mr John Fife on Monday noon gave a very good demonstration on the brain of the criminal who suffered on*

The Keelmen's Hospital on City Road in 1886, the scene of the murder. It was built by Newcastle's Keelmen in 1701 and was later administrated as a charity by the Corporation.

> *Saturday … Mr Fife … acquitted himself well in his place as lecturer, and had good opportunity, from the freshness of the brain before him, to exhibit its parts and structure in a clear manner, more than usually falls to the lot of an anatomical lecturer … The audience altogether might be about 50 of whom almost one third were non professionals.*

The court at the Guildhall, 1967. The fittings, including the spiked dock, are original, dating from the late eighteenth and early nineteenth century.

The Guildhall in 1829. Beyond, behind the tall warehouse and behind the crane, can be seen St Thomas's chapel.

There would have been little left of Jin by the time the medics had finished with her, but according to an old tale, something of her lives on. People passing the Guildhall would hear a disembodied voice singing one of the street traders' cries. The story doesn't explain why Jin, the former fish hawker, should change her calling in the afterlife and take up a fruit seller's song:

Fine Chinee oranges, four for a penny
Cherry ripe conberries, take them and try

When the jolly song was finished the voice pleaded 'Bring Billy Ellison to me'.

Perhaps Jin wanted to apologise to her lover for trying to send him to the gallows in her place.

Medics and students were admitted to the lectures free of charge, but it is obvious from Wright's journal entry, that anatomy lectures and dissections attracted considerable numbers of lay people, presumably wishing solely to satisfy their morbid curiosity. An advertisement for the lecture series states that for the sake of preserving order, all non-professionals were required to buy tickets, costing 2s. 6d. for a single lecture or 10s. 6d. for the course. This was expensive enough to deter many people and prevent crowds like those attending the trial and execution from ruining the scientific atmosphere of the lectures. Any profit from the series was donated to the eye hospital.

Most people would have been horrified at the thought of their mortal remains ending on the dissecting slab at the Barber Surgeons Hall, but occasionally someone came there of their own free will. A man called John Cutler made his living by selling pies to the medical fraternity. John Fife was so fascinated by Cutler's dreadful deformities that he offered him 10 guineas (in advance, of course) for dissection rights after his death. Cutler readily agreed. He reasoned that he had made a good living from the medics, so it would be only fair to give something back to them. And of course, 10 guineas was a small fortune.

A LIST OF
EXECUTIONS
IN NEWCASTLE-UPON-TYNE,
SINCE 1306.

DATE.	NAMES.	CRIME.	WHERE EXECUTED.	
1306 ————	John de Seyton	Prisoner of War	Hanged	Newcastle.
1461, May 1	James Butler, Earl of Ormond		Beheaded	do.
1464, — 15	The Earl of Kent		Beheaded	do.
1564 ————	Partrage	For Coining	Hanged	do.
1593, Jan. —	Rev. Edw. Waterson		Beheaded	Town Moor.
1594,	Rev. Thomas Boast		Hanged	do
1599, Aug. 22	Clement Roderforthe		do	in the Castle
1640, May 16	Two Soldiers	Denying the King's Pay	Shot	Newcastle.
1650, Aug. 21	14 Women, 1 Man, &	Witchcraft	Hanged	Town Moor.
	9 Moss Troopers	Robbery		
1701, Sept. 25	John Fenwick, Esq.	Murder	do	Newcastle.
1733, ————	Two Men		do	Town Moor.
1739 Sept. 4	Michael Curry and John Wilson	Murder	do	Westgate.
1743, Aug 8	Sir William Brown	Returning from Transportation	do	do.
1744. — 11	Thomas Lister	Horse-stealing	do	do.
————————	James Maben & John Samuel, for Coining		do	do.
1746, Sept 15	Alexander Anthony	Desertion	Shot	Town Moor.
1751, Aug. 21	Richard Brown	Murder	Hanged	do.
1752, Sept 27	Ewen M'Donald	Murder	do	do.
1754, Aug. 7	Dorothy Catinby	Murder	do	do.
1758, Feb. 8	William Bland	Desertion	Shot	do.
1758, Aug. 7	Alice Williamson	Burglary	Hanged	do.
1764, — 27	George Stewart	Murder	do	do.
1764, Sept. 3	James Edgar	Burglary	do	Westgate.
1776. Aug. 21	Robert Knowles	Stealing a Letter	do	Town Moor.
1776, — 21	Andrew M'Kenzie	Highway Robbery	do	Westgate.
1783, Nov. 17	William Alexander	Forgery	do	Town Moor.
1784. Aug. 27	James Chambers & William Collins	Robbery	do	do.
1786, — 30	Henry Jennings	Horse Stealing	do	do.
1790, — 5	Thomas Watson	Murder	do	Westgate.
1792. — 10	William Winter, Jane Clark, and Eleanor Clark	Murder	do	do.
1795, — 8	Thomas Nicholson	Murder	do	Town Moor
1805, — 16	Thomas Clare	Murder	do	Westgate.
1816, Sept. 7	James O'Neil	Highway Robbery	do	Town Moor.
1817, Dec. 3	Charles Smith	Murder	do	do.
1829, Mar. 7	Jane Jamieson*	Murder	do	do.
1844, Aug. 23	Mark Sherwood	Murder	do	do.
1850, — 24	Patrick Forbes	Murder	do	Gaol.
1863, Mar 14	George Vass	Murder	do	do.

* The Cost of Jane Jamieson's Execution was £28. 13s. 3d.

Newcastle-upon-Tyne : Printed and Sold by R. EMERY, Silver Street.

*A nineteenth century broadsheet detailing executions
in Newcastle 1306-1863, printed and sold by R.
Emery of Silver Street.*

Gaols, Gaolers and Gaolbreaks

From around 1400, Newcastle had two Gaols. Prisoners of the county were held in the Castle Keep, prisoners of the town authorities in the Newgate.

The Black Gate with the Keep beyond in 1931. The Heron Pit was situated to the left of the photograph behind the Black Gate. It was excavated in 1906. The ramshackle buildings of Castle Garth had been demolished by 1931, but even today there is a sinister atmosphere around this ancient structure.

The Heron Pit

In the Castle Garth is a dark, gaping pit, called the Heron Pit after the first governor, William Heron of Ford, Northumberland. Heron was a cruel and sadistic man with no sympathy for the prisoners in his charge. Prisoners were thrown into the pit through a trap door at the front of Heron's house. If they broke a limb during the descent, which could easily happen, there was no hope of medical attention. Prisoners could stay in the pit for months, even years, with no light and minimal food and would only be released if it suited Heron's whim.

The Guard Room

Prisoners of the Sheriff of Northumberland were tried in the castle hall (on the site of County Hall) and if convicted they were imprisoned in the guard room at the Keep. Prison reformer, John Howard was appalled when he visited the Keep in 1777. Prisoners were shackled to the wall in the dark and the place was cold and filthy. The castle roof had collapsed and water streamed down the walls into the dungeon. The sexes were allowed to mix freely, and at least one child had been conceived in the prison. On certain days, for a small charge, the public could visit the prison to gape at the entertaining spectacle of the degradation of their fellow humans.

The Guard Room in 1896, by which time it was no longer used as a prison.

Newgate

Newgate was the most important and impressive of the gates into the town, and with its barbican moat and drawbridge seemed impregnable. However, prisoners have plenty of time for creative thought, and many of them found ingenious ways of escaping, often through the sewers and chimneys. In the early 18th century a guardhouse was built in the south side of Newgate in an attempt to make the prison more secure.

All prisoners at Newgate were kept in irons because the gaol was so insecure. The prison was always overcrowded and male and female prisoners mixed freely. Each received an allowance of 5d (2p) a day, coals, a straw bed with ticking, one double blanket and one single, a rug and soap. They were allowed to use a common kitchen and to walk on the roof for exercise.

The Master Escapologist

Long before Harry Houdini thrilled audiences with his remarkable and daring escapes, Newgate had its own escapologist in the person of Thomas Tait. Tait worked as a turnkey at Newgate, but on June 8, 1736 he stole some cambric fabric from Mr Durance's shop in Newcastle. He made the mistake of giving a piece of the cloth to a godchild and unfortunately the child's mother tried to sell it back to Mr Durance. Tait was tried, convicted and imprisoned in his former place of work.

Of course, Tait had the advantage of knowing every corner of the gaol, but even so his feats were quite remarkable. On July 15, Tait and another prisoner, Alex Ogle, despite being chained to the wall, broke out of the prison. Accomplices were waiting in the toll shop where the prisoners' chains were removed. This should have been the point where Tait and Ogle fled the scene as quickly as possible. Instead they broke back into the gaol through the keeper's house, went to an upstairs room where Tait used to sleep before his crime. Although a sick servant was sleeping in the room, the men found Tait's clothes chest and dressed themselves in finery, and finally made their escape through the window, completely undetected.

Eventually Tait and Ogle were recaptured at Tait's sweetheart's house in Bellingam. When Tait was returned to Newcastle he boasted that there

was no point in chaining him again, because no chains could hold him. He then proceeded to prove it in front of two magistrates and a gaoler. In what must have been a spectacular demonstration Tait broke free of his bonds within fifteen minutes. The magistrates had Tait put under close guard until the next Assizes where he was sentenced to seven years transportation.

The Fat Felon in the Flue

On 2 March 1800, three prisoners, John Outerside, awaiting transportation, Richard Lowe, committed for forgery and Thomas Graham, committed for highway robbery tore their blankets into strips to make a rope, wrenched a bar from inside the chimney and climbed up. They tied their rope to a sundial on the roof, descended near Gallowgate and made their escape. Following them was a portly prisoner called John Sill. He stuck fast halfway up the chimney and had to stay there all night until the gaolers came to rescue him. According to some accounts, the flue had to be demolished before he could be released.

The Prison Pedestrian

At least one of Newgate's prisoners journeyed many miles without ever leaving the confines of the gaol. George Wilson was a celebrated pedestrian or distance walker. He had fallen on hard times and was imprisoned in Newgate for debt. On April 16, 1813, he agreed to attempt to walk 50 miles in under 12 hours. Of course, as a prisoner, his choice of routes was limited. He chose a small yard, measuring 33ft x 25ft 6 inches

The New Gate in 1789.

and walked around it more than 2,250 times to make up the distance. He completed his walk a mere 4 minutes and 43 seconds within the stipulated time. For this feat of endurance he earned £3 and 1 shilling, which seems an odd and rather trifling sum. Perhaps it was just enough to pay off his debts and secure his liberty.

When Newgate was demolished, some of the stones were incorporated in the new gaol, built in 1823 by John Dobson in Carliol Square.